Advance Praise

for Sarah Cortez's

How to Undress a Cop

"In this, her first collection of poems, Sarah Cortez has already found her voice and her subjects. The voice is brash and powerful and holds nothing back; and the poet commits herself wholeheartedly to depicting the joys of physical love and the risks of a dangerous profession. Cortez is unique: She leaves the reader with the tastes of both lipstick and metal in his mouth."

—Poet Robert Phillips,
author of *Breakdown Lane*

"Searing. Sexy. Stunning. Blunt. Sarah Cortez writes poems amazing in their life-force. Prepare to be startled."

—Poet and anthologist Naomi Shihab Nye,
author of *Hugging the Jukebox*

"Sarah Cortez brings a secret world into poetry, and her crafty first book— nervy, quick-hitting, street-smart, sexual—leaves each of us more startlingly aware of what we had overlooked, more keenly observant and acutely conscious."

—Poet Edward Hirsch,
author of *Wild Gratitude*

For Matthew, wishing you joy and grace in the words, Sarah Cortez

How to Undress a Cop

a Cop

Poems by

Sarah Cortez

Foreword by

Naomi Shihab Nye

Arte Público Press
Houston, Texas
2000

This volume is made possible through grants from the Andrew W. Mellon Foundation and the City of Houston through The Cultural Arts Council of Houston, Harris County.

Recovering the past, creating the future

Arte Público Press
University of Houston
Houston, Texas 77204-2174

Cortez, Sarah
    How to undress a cop / by Sarah Cortez.
        p.   cm.
    ISBN 1-55885-301-4 (pbk. : alk. paper)
    1. Mexican American women — Poetry. I. Title.
PS3553.O7227 H69 2000
811'.6—dc21   00-041636
                                                                CIP

CoolMax® and Kevlar® are registered trademarks of the DuPont Corporation (E. I. du Pont de Nemours and Company).

Acknowledgments may be found on page 80 and constitute an extension of this copyright page.

0 1 2 3 4 5 6 7 8 9   10 9 8 7 6 5 4 3 2 1

To my poetry-sisters—
Andrea, Anna, Brittney, Emma,
Jiwon, Joan, Judith, Mary, Mimi,
and Naomi

Contents

Foreword

I FIRST MET SARAH CORTEZ through her poems in the mail. She had applied to be part of a wonderful annual summer writing workshop for women in the Oregon wilderness called "Flight of the Mind."

Reading through a generous stack of applicants' manuscripts one midnight, I sat on the rug in my little writing room in San Antonio, swooning to the potent voices of women from around the country, not knowing how I could ever make the final selections for our class.

Boom!—there came Sarah. Her poems, with their tough muscles, neat lines, and rippling visceral imagery, woke me right up. I noticed she lived in Houston and wondered how I had never heard of her in my own state before.

Yes yes yes, I wrote in the margin. It was not only the rarity of police-world imagery in her poems that captured me, or the tantalizing, edgy sexiness discovered late at night, but an organic sense of narrative, a gripping rightness in how she shaped and layered a vivid scene. Many of her scenes made an eerie underworld feel very near. The intricate ways she wove dialogue, culture, and personal history into the tight bodies of her poems, created a provocative, highly charged atmosphere.

Of course we all learn early how a successful poem may translate us immediately out of our own scene into an intimate other, but it is always a revelation and a gift when it happens again.

Sarah seemed from the first as lively as her poems—strong, supple of heart, animated, interested in others. A small group of us set off on an excursion in Oregon one day, driving over the mountains, new friends telling life stories in the car. All of us marveled at Sarah's upbeat sensitivity, her deep alliance with so many worlds at once. It was hard to picture her in a police uniform; then again it wasn't. She was a person who would take risks that were worth it—writing, to her, was another kind of crucial risk. When she gave up police work a few years later to work full-time as a writing instructor, I had no doubt many other writers would benefit from her choice. Whatever world she inhabits will be a lucky one.

We celebrate this stunning debut, this contribution to the canon of Texas, to Latina literature, to the world of vigorous voices!

A year or so ago, Sarah Cortez came to San Antonio to read at the Public Library's "Copyright Texas" series. Afterwards, the coordinators said, "You didn't tell us she was rated R!" Well, she is. I am telling you now. You can handle it. But she is rated R for *risk* and *real* and *radiant* as much as for anything else.

Naomi Shihab Nye
San Antonio, 2000

How to Undress
a Cop

Hey, Ralph

Beginning at the skin
I want you.
On the hood of my patrol car,
legs spread,
ready and hard.
I'll be on top;
take what I need.
Send you back to work.
Then, call my dispatcher
and say, "In-service."

After Shift

You want me to come
to you each night, drop my gun belt,
lie along your muscled length,
bend when you decide, sleep
against your smudged tattoos,
your sprays of freckles covering me.

This is what you must provide—
sturdy legs to carry me tirelessly
into dreams. Strong arms to hold
out the night's shift work—
the four-year-old girl raped, the car
fire's human fuel, swollen, distended.

When you enter me, pierce
the oily film of peoples' lies,
fears, sadnesses I can't right.
Tell me your own policing stories.
Make it make sense. Remind me
there is no fairness, no justice.

Few heroes. Little hope.

If you can't, pretend.
Then lie to me and lie again.

Undressing a Cop

Do it first in your mind.
Many times. Linger over
details. Eye each piece
of shiny metal, thick black
leather, muscled bicep. Take

control when you start. Your
sure fingers will unhook
the square silver buckle
in front and listen to breath
change. You will unsnap keepers. Lower

gun belt to the floor while
unzipping Regulation trousers.
Before reaching inside, undo the
shirt's top button, unzip the front
flap hiding the chest. Kiss

underneath the badge's place. The silver
you've stared at—an engraved star
with blocked numbers that means your lover
may die for the State. Wonder what
it's like to be called by a number. Peel

back the shirt and drop it
on the floor. Pull up a V-necked white
T-shirt and suck the nipples, a surprise
of pink vulnerable flesh, alive, soft,
tender, bringing light into your mouth. Feel

the curve of rounded flesh
against your cheek. Lower your hands.
Tease the wet hardness aching inside
dark navy-blue trousers. Pick
a spot. Decide what you want.
Ride until you come. Don't try

to touch a heart or reach inside
guts. Instead, observe and maintain
the silence, your own backbone
rigid even while loving
and being loved.

Humberto

I long to be your girl
leaning on the blue Chevy's door.
With you, at sixteen,
standing, jacketed
against the dusk's purple
darkness, looking
into my eyes.

Listening to your soft *"Querida,"*
watching you light up like a torch
when I catch your gaze,
return a smile. Poking my finger
into the warm smooth spot
in your gaping shirt
where St. Christopher swings
golden and safe. My excitement
forbidden, concealed carefully
as a mother cradling a newborn
baby, who grows cold
too quickly even in the summer.

You'd walk me to classes. Your body
slightly turned towards me
even while we walked, dissolving
my concentration in your lily-white T-shirt
and carefully pressed pants. Long
muscles masked by dark brown skin.
You'd prove you were a man
as soon as you could, then
walk with a swagger.

I would have stayed
with you, been the wife,
had many babies
after loving in the dark.

This dream assails me.

By the Airport

There's been another Mexican
in my life. I don't remember
his name. Lean, tough, and older.
Aztec eyes. He worked by the airport
where we filled up the car
with gas. I'd just started driving
and I'd stop when the tank
was barely a quarter way gone.

He never spoke except about our Olds.
Once he laid on the floorboard
to check a fuse under the steering wheel.
I leaned over him at his order
to reach for the ignition.
I saw his dark eyes
hunt through the armhole
of my home-made summer dress, move
into the lace sheath of bra and slip.
I straightened up and went outside.
I will never forget the look he gave
me before getting up. My dress
wasn't enough; it wasn't there.

Su Hombre

I drove through your old neighborhood
today, where a boy rubs
the flat hardness of his stomach
into his girlfriend's belly,
pushing. She pushes back,
throws brown arms around his scarred neck
and head. Glances around to be sure
she's watched and arches into a thrust
of pelvis. Lays her entire length
against his upright, taut body.
Hard, ready, open, restless.

The other boys grin and wait.
They'll prove themselves men
soon enough on the cracked sidewalks
under the old leafy trees
in your neighborhood.

Su hombre.

Reunion

There is a new family at our reunion.
Descended from a girl who died bloody
giving birth. Her parents lying,
saying no baby survived,
throwing my grandfather off the land.

This new family is from the Valley.
Parched land, endless highways
greying into brown dust. The dream of water
shimmering silver below noon-high sun.
My new relatives. Three sons, one daughter
from that baby left by my grandfather, hurrying
out of Mexico into the States at sixteen.

Carlos. Javier. José. Martha. Three sons,
one daughter. José. The unmarried one
with pointed, snake cowboy boots, black
felt hat parked low on back of head.
A bandit mustache, silken and full,
hiding white teeth glistening strong
into easy smiles.

José. In a family
of men and women who love to dance
you dance every dance. Whirling
older aunts or teen nieces with grace.
Even your brother's toddler dances
with upraised, bent baby arms
holding your hands, circling
your palm legs and black boots.
Small-baby, blunt white leather shoes
dancing to your steps.

I speak to you at the picnic on Saturday,
looking into wide pools
of tinted sunglass covering half your face.
Your grin broadens, full blooms. I see
a black star high in the soft pink gum
of your mouth. None of the children
are yours. You work on cars.

Mi primo, I come to you full
of the city's rush and starts,
where I sit encased in glass
behind a metal desk. I seek
the earth's warm, brown curve
in your hug. Between your blackened fingernails
stubbing out Camels, I search. Beyond
the rusty barbed wire prongs
curling through the mounds of sand, along
the thin ridge of backbone curving into mattress, I
search. Smelling the dusty soil in your sweat,
embraced by the Naval tattoos
spliced across your muscles.

I want to enjoy you slowly
in the Valley's afternoon,
in a darkened bedroom, water-cooler angled
in the doorway, pink bedspread crumpled
on the floor. Before a rainstorm's heavy,
dust-laden drops hurl into parched earth.

Unfamiliar terrain. Where
passion becomes mother. Nourishment
from a man. You are
naked to the waist. Darkened chest,
scarred ribs, gaunt belly, hairless,
hairless. Black, laughing eyes.
Flat, sticker nipples.

Warm tortillas
fresh to eat
in a linoleum kitchen.

Stripped to belt buckle,
barefoot by the stove,
attending white dough rounds
of *masa* cooking, you laugh.

I wouldn't fit in here.
Where dark-haired, handsome men
come home for lunch every day,
babies crawling underfoot and precious.
Where women's shoulders are rounded,
soft and brown, for a man's fingers.

Mi primo, I look into my mirror,
I see you.

Foundations

This pair—the pink ones —
incised with a red heart and white Cupid's bow
came at Valentine's. These others,
frothed in coral lace with see-through V
of white eyelet, arrived at Easter.
Christmas brought golden thread
decorating smooth green satin —
a G-strap with thin black ribbons.

Who else do you know
who receives sexy underwear
from her Mom, girl cousins,
aunts, and nieces?

Gives it, too. In midnight blue silk
scattered with small pink rosebuds.
Or frilly red lace holding B-cups
sweet with satin pointelle.

It's an old family tradition,
I say to questioning *gringo* lovers.
Believe me,
it's an old family tradition.

Las Tías Speak

Las tías hint that she's pregnant.
Mi tío whispers that Alfred found her
with another man. To keep her
Alfred's marrying her today,
in front of a Baptist minister
whose tawny hair is marvelous
with hair spray and symmetry.

Carol walks to the front
of the Church, a tall statue
of blonde-gold, nineteen year old,
high-breasted, small-hipped beauty.
Her bouquet quivers, each
white, waxen flower fluttering
all the way up the aisle.
Her body trembles uncontrollably
especially during the whispered vows.
Will she fall? Can that stiff lace
dress hold her up? Is she after his money?

Cousin Alfred walks proudly erect
to his third or fourth blonde wife,
just like his brothers—astounding
record in our Catholic family. Each
thread in his gray silk suit is important.
Every black hair is trimmed, oiled, glossed
into place. Isn't he handsome!
Their mama is so proud—all her boys
went to college, all lawyers. All
good boys. I bet she doesn't even
speak Spanish. Can she cook?

Her fourth step-dad gives her away,
limping in a blue jean suit,
black desert flowers carved into his belt.
Her mother, tiny and dark, Mexican.
Short hair slicked into uneven patches.

Later I meet Alfred's pin-up girl.
She smiles and extends a hand,
no longer shaking. But her smile
goes no further than her teeth.
Could she be pregnant and still so slender?
Does she love him? How will their kids
learn Spanish? "Congratulations,"
I murmur, reaching to kiss
one flaxen cheek before bending down
in dutiful good-byes to embrace *las tías,*
black dresses tight across heavy arms.

Dream Man

I said, "He doesn't need to
speak English," to my girlfriend
as we joked, woman-to-woman,
discussing what some man
might do
as a lover. I said,
"As long as he knows
'*aquí,*' '*allá,*' '*ahorita,*'
and, of course, '*otra vez*'."
At which, she dissolved
into laughter. For after all,
we are modern women beyond
Catholicism, fresh tortillas at every meal.
Each, one husband already gone.

So, I said, "What is the name
of that *taquería* where you work
an extra job on Sunday nights?
Maybe, I'll find a *novio* there.
He's got to be Mexican."
She stopped. She paused.
She seriously said, "Oh, no, they're all
wetbacks. Right from Mexico. You don't
want one of those." I think
"Why not?" wanting a lapse,
a free fall into strong arms
streaked with sweat. A chest
smelling of fields. A man
whose thickened palms tenderly rub
a three-year-old's fat cheeks.

"Heal me," I whisper. Grant me
to stand again on cold linoleum watching
Grandma uncoil her thick grey braid.
Give me words to understand her
Spanish. Make love to me
on a white, cast-iron bed
as the outside calls to us—
steers bellowing, roosters,
the haunting swish of mesquite trees
on Grandfather's farm. Sleep
with me curled around pillowcases
Grandma embroidered and edged
with strong lace. Heal me. Heal me.
Make love to me and give me
a black-eyed child.

Dream

If I was a dark and beautiful man
this is what I would do.
Wear sharp red shorts
gathered at the waist. Run
around the park twice, every day,
and see my legs grow strong and thick.

I would shave every morning. The clean
stainless sweeping the contours of face, chin,
around moustache. I would rub
aftershave, cool, astringent
juice over jaws, chest,
arm-pits, stomach, crotch.

Loving women, I would choose
carefully. Prolonging the desire,
waiting, making myself wait. Coming
home to jerk off before bed.
Not choosing back seats, back
alleys, motels, parks, parking
lots. Waiting to be in her house,
where *la chica* lives. Watching
her sleeping breath before I leave,
knowing when she wakes she'll find
my scent in the morning's rumpled sheets
and remember.

I would be a good dancer. All the men
in my family are. Even *los viejos,*
bald, with rock-hard melon bellies.
I would clasp my beautiful cousins
close against the hardness of stomach and cock
at family reunion dances. And whisper,
"Prima," before I placed soft quick kisses
onto lipsticked smiles. Low sparking
desire careful in our eyes.

Finally, I would marry
a girl from my school. Beautiful,
with smooth brown skin,
long dark hair. She will go to Church
every Sunday. Give me children.
Raise them well. Fuss
when my newly polished shoes mark
the kitchen floor.

I will die an old man
in my favorite chair,
dreaming the high shallow V of geese
in the night clear sky.
Moustache whitened with age,
bristly staccato against dark
dark skin.

Driving Home

In front of a thunderstorm's ruckus
I drive fast, only slowing down
when I see a young Mexican who holds
a square orange flag on a skinny stick
for road construction. As if a neon
vest, work boots gummy with asphalt,
and wispy moustache could stop
even a small car.

My car is already at a standstill
but he keeps shaking that stick.
Flag jumping, skittering in front of
my car's bug-juiced bumper. I
recognize that movement—I've seen it
in bullfights when the matador dances
against hot death, teasing. Impatient
breath, black hair dappled in gore,
strong legs careening into unstoppable death.

Johnnie

You are the boy from Northside
I dated in high school. I remember
your heavy blue car
with smooth black seats
the coarse stitching uncomfortable
through a party dress.

You always wear a turtleneck,
white or black. Your dark face,
handsome face, an unsmiling icon
rising from its grip. Black,
oiled hair combed, every strand
in place. Careful excitement flickering
in your eyes. At stop lights
I see it. Measuring the route home
by the distance between our hands
on the car's immaculate front seat.

Your mom owns a bakery
in a part of town I don't go in.
One night we drive by it—
a large, white, clapboard house
painted with Spanish words
I can't read. It's dark
inside. Your mom doesn't wait up
for you. You never mention your dad.
You say the cops stop you
often, alone,
to see if you drive a stolen car.

You are so polite
always. You kiss me
goodnight in hard-lipped concentration.
Inside, I count the flowers
on my dress, knowing I
cannot want you. Unable to forget
you're a Mexican.

Lingo

This is how it goes
when you're dating
a cop.

You say, "Will you be home for dinner?"
He says, "Negative."

You say, "Do you like this dress?"
and he says, "It's a good visual."

"Face to face" is a meeting,
not a kiss or a snuggle.
"Fuck you" means hello.
"To dust" is to kill.

On Valentine's when I say
my bra size is 34B,
saying the "B" twice, so
the embarrassing "D" cup
won't be purchased, he
says, "Oh, yeah, 34 BRAVO."
I smile, hoping he'll find
a color lace I don't already have
under my own police uniform.

What isn't said is I love
you. Don't get shot tonight
on shift by a cop-hater. Don't die
before I die, alone
in an alleyway or on a bright street
in widening pools of blood.

Rosie Working Plain Clothes

She's a dish—that Rosie.
Half Mexican; half Irish.
Green eyes backed by a hell of a temper,
perfect peach skin and black curly hair.
Large breasts.

Rosie and I were standing together
in the females' locker room and,
you understand, I wasn't really looking at her chest,
but out of the corner of my eyes, I saw, I swear
to God, I saw her pull out from deep,
deep in her cleavage in the center of her pink lacy bra,
I saw her pull out an aluminum-finish,
eight inch long, nine millimeter, semi-automatic.
Then she pulled out one set of heavy-duty,
brushed stainless, Smith and Wesson handcuffs,
each side dangling from the other like an earring.
And then she pulled out her black plastic beeper,
and, my God, by this time I was staring. Flat-out
admiration. Complete and total fascination.
Oh, yes, that Rosie, she's quite a cop!

Applying to LAPD

The older guy sitting next to me drives Amtrak
trains in New Mexico. Suited in grey, lean-bodied,
he mentions his age in a confidential apology
for the craziness of trying for the finest PD
in America after sixteen years of railroad tracks.

He can't quit talking as we wait for the Oral
Board almost everyone fails. He hunkers down
into my polite listening and begins confiding
details about his prostate. I wonder if
excessive nerves always affect him this way.

The next day as our group prepares for the physical
agility tests, I tease an ex-Marine New Yorker about the size,
length, and weight of gold chains, gold anchors,
and crowned saints he's wearing on his broad chest.
Two hours later before pushups he tells me

how he combs his leg hairs all in one direction
sometimes—so they feel good. Then, how he trims
his underarm hair so it won't stick out in certain
shirts. Next, he confides he prefers trimmed pubic hair
so it won't all be in a wad as underwear comes down.

I itch to ask, "Yours or your girlfriend's?" But
I don't. Later, I sure wish I had found out
before he earns a shiny badge, gets his semi-automatic,
and has to back me up out on the streets.

Death

We never talk about it at work.
Although I have a manila folder
labeled "When I Die" in the top drawer
of my desk at home. All six
pallbearers chosen; all cops.

One afternoon another officer says,
"I don't even believe in God,"
as he pulls out a holy card
of St. Jude, explaining he's
the Saint of Lost Causes.

Next to us, the trained killer,
ex-Marine, shows us his three by four inch
New Testament carried in a plastic Zip-Lock
inside his shirt. It went overseas
with him. He laughs, "If I work, I have it."

I tell them about my Sacred Heart
of Jesus, painted rays of grace extending
gold and red from His hands on the rectangular medal
I wear pinned to my bra every shift. I brag
that I'm no longer Catholic. Hate the Church.

My manila folder has letters
for some friends. But, I haven't chosen
the music or decided about cremation.
My new boyfriend says, "You can't die."
He doesn't understand about being a cop.

Tuesday Afternoon Invite

A luxurious confession
in the deliberate eyes
of this man glancing downward
at my duty belt. Polished,
black leather, heavy, thick
and unyielding. He coaches
football, grew up somewhere
in the middle of America. Gold
glints in the fine hairs of arms,
backs of hands. Well-fed, clean-shaven.

He jokes, "You—only you —
can arrest me." I see his green eyes
widen above an easy grin
when I reply, "If I cuff you,
we ain't going back to the station."

He colors. From two feet away
I feel the heat rise
through his body. He turns
his back to me, offers
his large pale hands for the metal,
spreads his feet apart
like I'm sure he never did
playing collegiate football.
Impeccable, blonde haircut
inclined, waiting.

My buddy Juan gets shy
when I tell him
two guys last week
said they wanted to get laid,
handcuffs and all that.
"White guys," laughs Juan,
hunching his shoulders, still
big from high school football,
"they like their women aggressive."

Then he grins, showing off
his crooked teeth, "Not like us
Latinos that like our women
on the bottom
looking up into our eyes
like they need us."
He cradles an imaginary
swooning woman
as his ears pink,
and I think about
precision-cut blonde hair
above a starched collar.
A strong man wanting to be climbed.

Matinee

My regular partner's back
got hurt when some idiot
tried to run him over
on a traffic stop
and he had to fall
into a ditch fast-like.
I get assigned a new guy—
a transfer from Westside
with intense gold chains
licking down the front of his shirt
like they all wear
on that side of town.

I know he doesn't like women
because his eyes don't warm
up or focus when he talks to me
or any other female—not even
the perky civilians
in ponytails and tight rayon slacks
who work at the Station. I've heard
he's married. Maybe on his first
or fifth. Or between wives or
girlfriends, or just plain looking
because he doesn't wear a ring
and doesn't feel harnessed.

He dresses perfect
every goddamned shift. Not even
a smudge on his black boots.
Uniform shirt tailored to curve
around his biceps and his britches
tight enough to tell that he's circumcised
even in bad light. I'm still giving
him a chance to show me
he takes female officers seriously
even though he keeps trying to
maneuver me into doing all
the shift paperwork plus fueling the car.

I figure we're becoming a team
after we make it through
a couple of fights together
both of us rolling on the asphalt
trying to handcuff drunk
assholes, scarring up our leather,
and shouting directions at each other.
I'm getting to where I don't notice
his tight butt stuffed
into those deep blue trousers
which will bust out
if he goes over a fence
or into a dumpster.

The next shift we walk out
to our shop taking briefcases,
commenting on how the previous K-9
unit ate part of the back seat. He's
driving. He runs one big rancher's hand
over his perfectly symmetrical blonde hair-do
and lowers his freshly razored jaw
while peering into the rearview mirror.
He looks me straight in the eyes
after checking with Dispatch
and says, "No calls holding. Let's
go see an X-rated movie."

Tu Negrito

She's got to bail me out,
he says into the phone outside the holding cell.
She's going there tomorrow anyway for Mikey.
Tell her she's got to do this for me.

He says into the phone outside the holding cell,
Make sure she listens. Make her feel guilty, man.
Tell her she's got to do this for me.
She can have all my money, man.

Make sure she listens. Make her feel guilty, man.
Tell her she didn't bail me out the other times.
She can have all my money, man.
She always bails out Mikey.

Tell her she didn't bail me out the other times.
I don't got no one else to call, cousin.
She always bails out Mikey.
Make sure you write all this down, cousin.

I don't got no one else to call, cousin.
I really need her now.
Make sure you write all this down, cousin.
Page her. Put in code 333. That's me.

I really need her now.
Write down "Mommie." Change it from "Mom."
Page her. Put in code 333. That's me.
Write down "Tu Negrito." Tell her I love her.

Write down "Mommie." Change it from "Mom."
I'm her littlest. Remind her.
Write down "Tu Negrito." Tell her I love her.
She's got to bail me out.

A Certain Kind of Case

My buddy Danny says, "You can't work
those kinds of cases your whole career. It changes
you. You have to watch videos.
Hours and hours. You have to understand

how they think." I realize I'd never thought
of it—who worked those cases, who
they went home to and what their wives fixed
for dinner. How they fell asleep, still thinking

about those tapes. Danny shakes his head
back and forth, disbelieving. "It takes at least five
years for an investigator to get good. You have to learn
certain terms they use among each other. Once

we did a search warrant at a pedophile's house. Less than
five minutes after the tape's delivery and it was
already in his VCR. Trash knee-deep inside. Piled high
in every room of his house, except the closet

where he kept his films and books. Totally
clean. Dust-free. Labeled by category in precise block
letters. Alphabetized like a library. We had to wear
overalls, gloves, and boots to walk through
half-eaten rotting food in wrappers."

Francisco

Arrested on an outstanding warrant,
he's pudgy, Mexican, and dead drunk.
Indecent exposure. Who would want to see?
Named Francisco, twenty-two years old.

He's pudgy, Mexican, and dead drunk;
he can't focus his eyes.
Named Francisco, twenty-two years old,
retching across the smooth back seat.

He can't focus his eyes
when my trainee handcuffs him
reaching across the smooth back seat.
I want this over with.

When my trainee handcuffs him
I stay clear of coughed-up cheese.
I want this over with
before we reach the jail.

I stay clear of coughed-up cheese
feeling sorry for all of us.
Before we reach the jail
he is fighting.

Feeling sorry for all of us
the jail deputies haul him away.
He is fighting;
I hear Francisco choke.

The jail deputies haul him away,
blood splattering from his mouth.
I hear Francisco choke.
I see bright drops cluster near his toes.

Blood splattering from his mouth,
he fingers a loose tooth, puzzled.
I see bright drops cluster near his toes.
Indecent exposure. Who would want to see?

To Another Officer

I remember the night the call came.
You were the primary unit. I checked by.
The suspect was 99-D. Then, actors on the ground.

These words can't carry the bluish glint of a gun
pulled out of a puckered waistband, the smell
of your aftershave, or the yellowish hue of his ragged teeth
trying to bite us. Wrestling, trying to remember,
remember if I was ready to die.

We did good. We cuffed him and no one got hurt.
I didn't want to hold a slender finger in a bullet hole
in your guts all the way to the hospital
like I did last week for another officer.

Wounded

We sit watching
videotapes about murderers.
Training from the Feds—
how to read blood splatter,
conduct investigations, figure out
if the homicide is organized
or disorganized, anger or power
related, done by a stranger
or a friend.

Each officer stares
at the TV thinking,
I hope to work one.
Catch the suspect. Put him
behind bars forever
or watch him fry.

That night I still remember the photos—
the fourteen-year-old girl
before he killed her. Sitting naked,
wearing a silver choke collar, hair
shorn to display her. Full breasts,
bruised. Will I ever see my own body
without seeing her, feet up,
staring with bleak eyes
into his Polaroid camera?

Silenced

At the signal, all officers stand saluting.
Stiff arms and spines, each badge covered
with black ribbon. Row after row, in ranks
from many departments we stand. Gossip
stilled. We listen to the volleys of gunfire,
the loneliness of "Taps" on winter air.

I've never seen police officers cry
but it's all I hear as we stand at attention
sniffling, clearing throats, sobbing
out the pain and loss from gullets
accustomed to holding it in,
choking it down, going about
other business all day, into night.

Late Night *Torta*

I won't take you
as a lover
unless you eat with me
at my favorite *taquería.*

I have to see you
crunch into *jalapeños,*
smell vinegary *comino* seeds,
sink teeth into carrot wheels
tasting like fire.

I want to see your nostrils
flare before biting
into a *torta.* Inhaling
sultry garlic seeped with
tomato inside the meat.
A dark layer of *frijoles*
cushioning crisp, thin-cut lettuce.
White *crema,* sassy and rich.

Your lips will redden
from the *salsa.* Faint sweat
will bead above your moustache.
I will watch the tattoos on your arms
swim above your ungiving muscles
in the bright pink and green lights.

The Virgen on the cash register table
will smile behind
her dark Indian eyes. She has
an angel to lift her
with his wide-flighted wings.
As you will lift me later
with your tongue.

Cruising

in my boyfriend's car, listening to loud music, I hear
my cousin ask, *"Prima,* are you wearing enough mascara?"

I flip down the turquoise visor's mirror
hunting in my purse for glossy Lash Lengthener.

Meantime, Américo guns the engine
because he gets a kick out of black lines streaky

down my face. I smolder him a look
so he knows he ain't getting it in the back

seat tonight. The white knife scars
on his cheeks glow like lace doilies.

I want to lick them but it'd really turn him on
and it's way too early. He feels my heat and slides me down

to his shoulder. *"Ruca,"* he whispers,
tilting his pelvis upward, while I finger his new, crusty tattoos.

"Ay, hombre," I joke, handing my mascara to my cousin
in the back seat with her man. I grab at her lipstick, while longing

for sin. "Later," I say, smoothing the white, stretched jersey
over my dark and beautiful breasts, waiting for my desire to match his fire.

My heart like the Virgin's in *Abuelita*'s picture—studded with small flames,
holding skinny brown arrows, exposed, glowing and full of crazy loves.

Devour

I run for your belly,
eat out your heart,
gorge on your jowl.
Lap the glistening blood
pushing through stomach,
guts, and groin.

Inside of you, I drink
red and more red
until its pulsing fills
my ears and fevers
my own mixed blood.

Poets call this Love;
I name it
Hunger.

Glance

Your eyes liquid
at the sight of me.

I jump in.

Chulo

It's time for a young lover.
One with a lean waist disappearing
into low-slung trousers. No belt,
unshined shoes. He drinks a *raspa*
for breakfast, while driving to work.

Around his left bicep is a Crown
of Thorns, tattooed in navy-blue ink.
He isn't losing his hair and doesn't pay
ex-wives. He smiles easily;
life is simple. He keeps his hair
too short and jokes that girls like to
bed "bad boys." I remind him
that a real woman won't waste time
with one of those and he grins,
then walks flat up to my face,
straightens up his slouch,
imprints his taut stomach
into my belt buckle, smiles again,
and says, "I'm ready."

I move aside the dark-brown scapula.
Its holy image riding the crush of felt
and knotting. Beneath it I touch
your lean chest, your back. I find
La Virgen de Guadalupe lying in pools
of your hot muscle. This is all I want
from you—a narrow bed, angled pelvis,
a few nights. A walk across
empty streets. Your slenderness
a torch, calling me further
further.

Her

She has white skin.
This new girl of yours;
freckles too.

I bet she wears
white cotton underwear
that leaves puckered bands
of pink welts when she strips
for your waiting mouth.

I bet she doesn't snore
or drool hot threads of mucus
into the sheets which cool
as stale claws across her cheek.

Or do you two stay up nights?

Laughing at your good fortune,
squeezing yellow Parkay
on hot popcorn.

The First Time

I admire the pretty color
carpeting. I see a square
stainless, two-hole toaster
on the floor. One fine, old,
wooden chest-of-drawers facing
the only door.

When I feel the warmth
of his thick arm around
my neck from behind
and his beautiful lips meandering
up my earlobe, I grab hold
of that arm. My own hand—
large and strong—can't encircle
his muscles against my collarbone.
His breathing deepens, slows.

Will this be the place?
On this mattress, lopsided
across a rayon cover
that I will be raped?
I should not have sat
on the bed. Shouldn't
have met for coffee. He goes
to Church every Sunday and Wednesday;
he adores his mom.

This may be the place.
On a Saturday afternoon
by a man
in an ordinary apartment
above a sea-green ocean
of new carpet
and uncertain, greying light.

Surprise Visit by Thirteen-Year-Old

When I ask your name
I expect "Roberto"; I get
"Robert". We sit on the couch
looking through the stack of postcards
you asked to see. Half-way down
there's a 1945 photo-card of an arrested
transvestite. Then, after purple Monet
water lilies, a young Marilyn squeezed
into a '50s corseted swimsuit
by a wardrobe matron. Above her small waist
her breasts rise like blown glass
over the contoured edge of Puritan spandex
restraint. You say quietly, "Marilyn,
she looks nice." I flip
hurrying to safer subjects—abstract
art, city silhouettes against impossibly-colored
sunsets. We reach a 1930s set
of stockinged legs in pumps with rhinestone
heels. Seams of fishnet snake up,
centered into plump warm flesh.
A bare bottom crowns the vista. You
ask, "Do you dress like that?" I
have to make it funny. I laugh
as if I hadn't already noticed
your hair curling around your ears,
the tender nape of your neck, and the
pristine white socks covering your calves.
I laugh a silly giggle, and say,
"No, never."

Benediction

My mind goes into doorways
it shouldn't sometimes
when I'm alone. I dream
two thumbs hooked
jerking down underwear.
A mouth searching
for my tight bud
furled star
nestled in folding,
fleshy gates
between my thighs.
A blessing
on this flat earth.

Bouquet

I pause on the way
out the door. Give you
a look that says
rich dark fruit
between my legs
for you to eat. My
thighs a flower
of pale longing.

Opening, opening,
offering, accepting.

It is springtime, my love.
Come here. Undress me
in the flowers. Eat me
in the sun. Smell
my love for you
in the springtime,
my love.

Rain

In the early morning
you turn towards your wife. With
grey raindrops drumming
on the roof, you touch at
her shoulder and the pink
strap falls. Before the kids
awake, with the door closed,
you jerk your briefs
to your knees. She turns.
You reach beneath the chiffon folds
of her Mother's Day gown,
squeeze, reaching for the softness
with your penis, to enjoy.

Song of Love

Gleaming, gold chains circled your thick,
muscled neck. A heavy, linked bracelet
cuffed your wrist. We snuck away
during the luncheon to the hotel
room overlooking City Hall.

I watched you unzip your trousers,
lower jacquard silk boxers,
pull your thickness into your right hand,
and love yourself. The strong pinkness
bent into your palm's knowing steady caress.
Your gold bracelet jingled against the diamond Rolex.
Metal against metal, intricate golden friction,
your song of love.

Troth

What do we offer each other
ultimately, except our beliefs?
After coupling, after the first five
years, when the usual becomes boring,
what makes us feel in the right place?

The world is flat. You laugh
at me. *A man past forty*
is no good in bed. I find out
much later how wedded you are
to this lie.

Both of us believe some few things.
Symphony on Sunday afternoons
in dress-up clothes. To sleep
curled around each other every night.
Cooking with fresh herbs; dinner parties.

But these sharings don't hold us
together. You're gone, husband.
The one time I telephone you to say,
"I forgive you for stopping
your love for me," you say,
"Don't call me ever again,"
and I believe you.

Mystery

I look at the pairs of people. Some
mystery contained between them.
The hand inserted in a pocket
for money before the other asks.
The careful pause, however slight,
for the other's rounded belly
when there's no room
for both to fit with ease
through a narrow doorway
or between a heavy chair and its table.

What is the glue holding people
together? It can't be passion.
I don't believe it's curiosity.
Surely not beauty, or lies,
or mere habit. If I knew
I'd give it to you and to me
like a bitter dose out of a blue bottle
to seal us together
to make us one
for a blessed eon.

Instructions

for Toi

Get a small crucifix. Make sure
it's real gold, so your neck
won't turn green. You'll be sweating.

Lace is very important. Buy it
in bright colors to cradle
your luscious breasts and firm butt.

Your jeans must hold your cheeks
tighter than any old-fashioned lover. Before
they zip, your tummy will bulge through and across
at least three inches. Suck it in and don't sit down.

Your brother home from the Marines will polish
your cowboy boots and they don't go on 'til
you're out the door. The glide of foot into leather
the only time you'll bend over tonight.

Walk like you're in control. Feel yourself
get wet when you strut. Remember, the boys know
this too. Check them out. You'll see
it in the fronts of their Wranglers.

Choose your hat very carefully. Black felt
after September one; straw when summer comes.
Know where every strand of hair lies. Use gel,
hair spray, or mousse—as long as the wind won't move it.

Spray perfume everywhere—hair, armpits, neck,
cleavage, the front of your jeans where the zipper closes.
Do your nails bright red like a Camaro's tail lights.
Let your sister help—three coats mascara, four of lipstick and liner.

Taste a man's pungent aftershave
against your pink tongue and see his blunt fingers
scrape down your bra as the pickup's windows cloud over.
You'll choose the one you want and have him many times.

On the way out the front door, your Mamá will tell you
you're going straight to hell and your brother will offer
to kill any boy who messes you around. You'll run
one hand over the abundant curve of your right hip
dreaming of all the loving you will try to hold.

Fully Equipped

See this thin black ribbon rimmed
in gold, embroidered with Latin
words meaning *Don't forget me.*
Not ever. Exact revenge.

Sold in police equipment
catalogues on pages marked
"Miscellaneous." Available in packs
of three, or half a dozen.

The first time I used black vinyl
electrical tape. Next time, I borrowed one
from a lanky, career lieutenant
who fastened it with velcro squares.

Now I buy my own for another
funeral. Officer shot in the neck
by a seventeen-year-old male. I strap it
across my silver badge, a star saddened.

Training Photos

A butter-colored handful
of intact convoluted mazes—
a human brain blistering on hot cement.
A summer afternoon. Motorcycle

wreck. Half the block's length
black squiggled burns of rubber.
He hit a curb. Lost control.
Hit another curb and died

just after. Leaving bright scabs
of blood, that small section
of brain, a black boot with silver
squared buckle. His mouth grins,

discolored teeth devouring pavement.
Wispy hair a mat of oily straw. Half
a bag of dope stuffed in his right
sock. No helmet, nineteen

years of age. No striking vehicle.
He lost control. Maybe, forgot
how to brake or was thinking
of a big night to come, or one just ended.

Flag-Down

The temperature is, at least,
105 degrees Fahrenheit. A man
waves me down from
a waxed black Cadillac.

He's yelling and gesturing. I
figure someone is in danger
or has been hurt. A heart attack,
stroke, knife, or guns.

I brake my shop and approach
the driver's side window. He
shrieks, "Did you see it? Did
you see it?" Finally he gasps,

"A bird. A large bird. It's hurt—
walking on the ground." I tell
the dispatcher I'm looking for a large bird
and out-of-service for other calls.

My dispatcher can't hide the giggle
in his voice. A wrecker-driver buddy
drives over in case we need to winch it
up. I can't locate the bird

who is clearly smarter than any of us
walking around in this heat. But, later
I drive by and see a splattered mass of feathers
splayed against a curb, pinions askew,

head a band-aid on the heated cement.
Caught in a surprise, a white breast
leaking blood onto pavement. Feathers
a flurried band of astonishment.

Ode to Body Armor

Sturdy, lightweight, space-age Kevlar,
miracle of modern technological advancements,
mysterious fusion of high tenacity fibers encircling
my heart, lungs, and guts. Protect me against
the bullets of those who wish to kill me. Guard

the rich red juice, flowing veins, arteries. Remember
you meet National Institute of Justice requirements
for wet and dry ballistics. Your threat level is IIA.
You extend coverage over the three inches of ribs
so I can't be drilled sideways. Pray, deflect

bullets caught on your edge away from vital
body organs. Coax and call me to wear you
on summer days when I can't breathe' for the heat,
and sweat sluices inside your flex-hard shell. Let

me be the one to live. To keep shooting.
May I be the one pictured grinning in color ads
saying, "Bruised but alive." Oh sweet
sweet ballistic vest with adjustable Velcro straps,
trauma plate, and CoolMax carrier liner, save me.

Bring me home out of darkness.

Convenience Store Call, Mid-Shift

I stand cradling a beige business phone
next to a stand-up dairy case
of frozen snacks. The thick window
on top invites secretive glances, desire
coated with nuts ready for icy tonguings.

My boyfriend gripes about his Sgt.,
yells at his partner, describes busting
in a door on a felony warrant tonight,
and tells me what he ate for lunch.
I say, "I'm thinking about you."

I stare at hand-held, several-inched, thick delights
named "Big Shot," "Drumstick," or
"Husky." Glittering ice surrounds
promises for ecstasy of taste, creamy sweetness,
or a cherry center ringed by nuts. I tell my man,

"Wait up for me and wear that cologne."

Interlude

I watch a handsome young female
heifer along a ditch line, tramping
down knee-high weeds, tail swishing. Ears
outlined against the blaze of car headlights
at sixty miles per hour. She's free—
she's an 800-pound potential traffic hazard.

An off-duty cop pulls up in a shiny, red,
one-ton, extended cab pickup. Shirtless
because he's been mowing fields on a tractor.
She's too spooked to come to his horn
or be roped. He tries to help me out
but the cream-colored, good-looking heifer won't respond.

Waiting for the Livestock Officer, we talk
standing. He crosses his arms over
his bare chest, deepening the crease
between his tits, the beckoning seam of dark hair.
I focus on his eyes, chin, moustache—
anywhere higher than his chest.

Anywhere safer than the tanned stretch
of smooth stomach sliding into dark green twill
shorts. He gives me his name and shift,
days off, cell phone, pager, extra job
location. The owner of the cow arrives,
Marlboro dangling inside the smooth sweep

of her burgundy Buick. I disregard the Livestock
Officer. The cow gets roped, her adventure
ended. He leaves grinning on the other side
of his naked chest, briefly lit by speeding headlights,
a scant outline against black twilight's pliable face.

For Kathy

I fan breath
on your shoulders'
skin, against
bones, into freckles.

You murmur
and wait for me
to climb over
and on top.

We reach to
one another
slowly, slowly
inside prior

hauntings.

Attempt to Locate

Bebopping into Juarez
hot sun on our heads,
Mary, Raúl, and I are walking
fast. Me in front, Raúl
almost keeping up, courtesy
of Army Reserves twice monthly. Mary's
lagging because she's not yet fit
after her on-duty back injury.

We're joking about being three
police officers walking into
a country not famed for justice
or mercy, when I see in the front
window of a shop, beside a lavender
lace bra and an infinite array
of sheer, pastel, nylon panties,
a clothing item I can't figure out.

Huge silver sequins cover
two triangular pieces of fabric.
A delicate beige band holds it
all together. I think BRA—
a Border version! I reach for
Raúl's arm as he breezes by,
buzz-cut hair obstinately forward,
growling, "I don't do lingerie."

By now, Mary has caught up and I grab her
instead, also just now figuring out
this is a garter belt. "Look, Mary,
there are sequins, so the guys can
find it in the dark."

We each see our dark triangle
framed by huge, round, silver sequins,
illuminated in reflections of neon
Border lights, on top of a strong man
in a hotel room, flushed and sweating.

Then my 4' 6" friend, who entered the Marines
when no girl did that, who now raises a son
alone after two spent marriages,
who lives with her Mom, who goes to Church
cada día, and is taken seriously on the streets
in uniform, says, "You know, most of those guys
need lights and sirens to find it too!"

Anew

Small yellow flowers out back.
A white rabbit eating bark.
An unnamed part of me
wants to claim untouched
again. The early years

before the one touch
opened me, diverted my blood.

Now I lie beneath your weight.
The press and heaving, a new
friction beyond girlish dreams.
Your thick waist, rough chin, wet
breath against my listening ear.

I long to be vestal. Slender
as a boy. Unmarked, hopeful,

bloodied and afraid.

Index of First Lines

Index of First Lines

Acknowledgments

The following poems first appeared in the periodicals noted: "After Shift," in *Louisiana Literature*; "A Certain Kind of Case," in *Louisiana Literature*; *"Chulo,"* in *MA-KA* (Sister Vision Press, Toronto); "Death," in *The Texas Observer* and in *WomenPolice*; "Dream," in *Plural Desires* (Sister Vision Press, Toronto); "Her," in *Chiron Review*; "Interlude," in *The Bayou Review*; "Johnnie," in *Tex!*; "Lingo," in *The Midwest Quarterly*; "Reunion," in *Plural Desires* (Sister Vision Press, Toronto); "Rosie Working Plain Clothes," in *Tex!*; "Silenced," in *WomenPolice*; "To Another Officer," in *Rogue's Gallery*; *"Training Photos,"* in *Blue Violin*; *"Tu Negrito,"* in *The Texas Observer*; "Tuesday Afternoon Invite," in *Louisiana Literature*; and "Wounded," in *The Texas Observer*.